W9-BDV-670

Dutch!

COOKING UNLIMITED

Yes, of course there is real Dutch cooking! In fact, this book is too small – we had lots more authentic Dutch dishes. We finally made this selection for the simple reason that these dishes are delicious and easy to prepare.

Despite strong influences from other countries, the Dutch haven't lost their taste for mashed potatoes and cabbage, main course soups and filling desserts. Pasta from Italy, sushi from Japan, tapas from Spain and wok dishes from Asia make wonderful additions to our own tasty dishes.

This book will ensure we don't forget the traditional recipes for rice pudding, or how to make chips yourself or even put together a small rijsttafel (rice table). You are bound to find a recipe that takes your fancy; Dutch cooking unlimited!

traditional Dutch snacks & meals

Bitterballen (type of croquette served as an appetizer) . . . 8

Kaas uit het vuistje (cheese cubes) . . . 10

Hollandse nieuwe (Dutch early-season herring) . . . 12

Chips with mayonnaise . . . 14

Sandwich with peanut butter and hagelslag (chocolate sprinkles) . . . 16

Hutspot (stew) with rib of beef . . . 18

Meat balls and gravy . . . 20

Kale and sausage . . . 22

Pea soup with rye bread and smoked bacon . . . 24

Donder en hete bliksem (potatoes, apples and ham) 26

Zeeland mussels 28

Dutch rijsttafel (rice table) 30

traditional Dutch desserts & pastries

Pancakes with syrup 34

Mini pancakes with icing sugar 36

Haagse bluf (red currant whip) 38

Butter biscuit 40

Wentelteefjes (French toast) 42

Rice pudding 44

traditional Dutch snacks & meals

makes approx. 28 balls

125 g butter
125 g flour
400 ml beef stock
nutmeg
200 g cooked shredded beef
egg yolk
4 tbsp. of cream
50 g flour
4 beaten egg whites
150 g bread crumbs
oil for deep frying
coarse-grain mustard
salt and pepper

Bitterballen

(type of croquette served as an appetizer)

Melt the butter and stir in the flour. Cook this for 2 minutes.
Add the beef stock and stir well until a smooth ragout is formed.
Add nutmeg, salt and pepper to taste. Stir in the meat, the egg yolk and cream. Put the ragout in the refrigerator for at least 2 hours, preferably overnight so that it becomes firm.
Make 28 small balls from the cold ragout and roll them in the flour, the egg white and the bread crumbs. Then roll them in the egg white again and finally in the bread crumbs once more. Shape the mixture into neat balls and leave to firm up for another 30 minutes in the refrigerator.
Heat the oil to 180 °C and deep fry the bitterballen until golden brown. Drain on paper towels and serve with (coarse-grain) mustard.

Kaas uit het vuistje

(cheese cubes)

The Dutch love to snack on little cubes of cheese. Serve the cheese cubes on a wooden board with cocktail sticks and serve with mustard, gherkins and cocktail onions.

To make cheese you need milk. Young cheeses, such as fromage frais and kwark (curd cheese), are unsalted and made without pressing, whereas cheeses that are salted and shaped have rennet added to them. Once in the correct shape, the ripening process can commence. The time required depends on the kind of cheese and its size. The quantity of liquid in the curd also determines the kind of rind or mould that forms on the cheese. The rind has a big advantage for the buyer. It not only protects the cheese, but you can tell the type of cheese from its rind.

The Dutch are very good at making cheese. Most foreigners have heard of the Alkmaar cheese market and of Gouda cheese, that they generally pronounce as 'gooda'.

The herring season starts mid May and runs until March. Most of the herrings caught are processed into other products, while 20% of the catch is processed into salted '*maatjesharing*', which is young herring. *Maatjesharing* are herrings that have never spawned.

Hollandse nieuwe

(Dutch early-season herring)

'Vlaggetjesdag', originally the Saturday before Whitsun, is the day when the arrival of the *nieuwe haring* is 'celebrated' in Scheveningen harbour, with the ships and harbour decorated with flags. The first barrel of 'new' herrings is sold by auction on a day prior to Vlaggetjesdag. The proceeds are donated to charity. Vlaggetjesdag has lost its original meaning due to new fishing methods and the use of different kinds of ships.

Pickled herring is herring that has been pickled in vinegar. It is made from herrings caught after June because these fish are too fat to be used for Hollandse nieuwe. A rollmop is a rolled herring with a piece of gherkin in it. The roll is held together with a cocktail stick and pickled in vinegar. The Dutch like to eat Hollandse nieuwe with chopped onions with their hands. Pick up the herring by the tail, pass it through the onions and hold it above your mouth and take a bite.

serves 4

Chips with mayonnaise

750 g chipping potatoes
salt
oil for frying
mayonnaise

Peel the potatoes, cut them into chips and dab them dry.
You can also buy special chip cutters in good household shops.
Heat the oil to 160 °C and fry the chips in small portions for 4 minutes until they are light in colour. Drain them on a paper towel.
Heat the oil to 180 °C and finish frying the chips in larger portions for 4 minutes. Drain them on a paper towel and sprinkle them with salt. Naturally, they are best served with real mayonnaise.

Sandwich with peanut butter and hagelslag (chocolate sprinkles)

makes 4 sandwiches

8 slices of bread
butter
4 tbsp. peanut butter
4 tbsp. chocolate sprinkles *(hagelslag)*

The Dutch sometimes like to put together unusual combinations of flavours. Who hasn't tried bread with cheese and sambal or bread with cheese and syrup or jam? But what really amazes foreigners is a sandwich with peanut butter topped with hagelslag (chocolate sprinkles). Of course, hagelslag is typically Dutch, so even hagelslag on its own makes heads turn.

Spread the slices of bread with butter and spread 4 with peanut butter. Sprinkle hagelslag on the top and cover with a second slice of bread. Cut the sandwich in half.

serves 4

Hutspot (stew) with rib of beef

500 g rib of beef
1 kg potatoes,
peeled and quartered
800 g carrots,
peeled and finely chopped
2 large onions,
finely chopped
50 g butter
2 onions, coarsely chopped
salt and pepper

Boil the rib of beef for at least 2 hours in a pan with plenty of salted water. Take the meat out and put the potatoes in the same pan with the remaining cooking liquid. Add the carrots and onions and cook for 20-30 minutes until the potatoes are cooked.
In the meantime melt the butter and fry the onions. Add water to make a good gravy. If required, add a dash of soy sauce to give more taste. Shred the meat and stir it into the gravy. Mash the hutspot with a potato masher. If necessary add a knob of butter and a dash of milk and season with salt and pepper. Divide the hutspot between the plates and add a generous spoon of meat and gravy.

serves 4

Meat balls with gravy

500 g lean mince
1 onion, finely chopped
1 egg
1 tbsp. paprika
1 tbsp. tomato ketchup
1 tsp. mustard
3 tbsp. bread crumbs
50 g butter
salt and pepper

Mix the mince with the onion, egg, paprika, tomato ketchup, mustard, bread crumbs, salt and pepper, and form into 4 large balls. Melt the butter in a frying pan and brown the balls all over. Fry gently for 12-13 minutes until they are cooked, turning them regularly. Take them out of the pan and keep them warm.
Add some water to the frying fat and stir round the bottom of the pan. Put the balls in the gravy.

serves 4

Kale with sausage

1 kg potatoes,
peeled and quartered
1 tsp. salt
1 kg kale, washed and
finely shredded
smoked sausage
knob of butter
dash of milk
1 gravy packet

Parboil the potatoes in water with a small amount of salt. Put the kale in with the potatoes and boil until the potatoes are cooked.
For the last 5 minutes put the smoked sausage on the kale.
Strain the potatoes with the kale. Mash the potatoes and kale together, and add butter and milk to make a puree.
Make up the gravy according to the instructions on the packet.
Place the kale on the plates, make a hole in the centre for the gravy and add the slices of smoked sausage.

Pea soup with rye bread and smoked bacon

serves 4

500 g soup meat
500 g green split peas
1 tsp. pepper
1 large onion, roughly chopped
3 leeks, in small pieces
1 celeriac, in small blocks
2 winter carrots, sliced
2 meat stock cubes
celery leaf, roughly chopped
1 smoked sausage
8 slices of rye bread
100 g smoked bacon
1 tbsp. mustard
salt and pepper

Put the meat, split peas, pepper, onion, leek, celeriac, carrot, stock cubes and celery leaf in a large soup pan and add 2.5 l water. Bring this to the boil and let the pea soup simmer gently for 4 to 5 hours. Stir regularly.

Take the meat out of the soup and remove rind and bones. Cut the meat into small pieces and return to the pan. Cut the smoked sausage into slices and put in the soup. If required, mash the pieces of vegetables with a fork. Season the soup with salt and pepper. Serve the pea soup with rye bread, slices of smoked bacon and mustard.

serves 4

1 kg potatoes, peeled and quartered
750 g apples, peeled and in pieces
knob of butter
dash of milk
8 slices of boiled ham
salt and pepper

Donder en hete bliksem

(potatoes, apples and ham)

Parboil the potatoes in a pan with a small amount of water and salt. Put the apples in the pan and finish cooking the potatoes. Drain off the boiling water and mash the potatoes and apples together with a masher. Make a puree with butter and milk and season with salt and pepper.
Divide between 4 plates and put the slices of ham on top.

Zeeland mussels

serves 4

2 kg mussels
2 tbsp. olive oil
1 onion, coarsely chopped
1 leek, in rings
1 carrot, in half slices
200 ml dry white wine
salt and pepper

Rinse the mussels under cold running water. Remove the beards and throw away any broken mussels or ones that are already open. Put the mussels in a large pan and add the onion and carrot. Pour the wine on them, sprinkle with salt and pepper and put the lid on the pan. Boil the mussels for about 8 minutes until they open. Any mussels that remain closed should be thrown away. Delicious served with French bread or chips and mustard mayonnaise.

serves 4

Dutch rijsttafel

(rice table)

300 g rice
4 tbsp. olive oil
300 g chicken filet, in cubes
1 tbsp. chicken spices
1 packet of satay sauce
150 g ham, in cubes
1 leek, in rings
1 sachet of dry nasi herbs
7 eggs
prawn crackers
gherkins and cocktail onions
sambal oelek

Boil the rice according to the instructions on the packet, drain it and leave it in a pan with the lid on.
Heat 2 tbsp. olive oil and fry the chicken filet until browned all over.
Season with chicken spices and fry the chicken for 6-7 minutes.
Prepare the satay sauce according to the instructions on the packet and stir the chicken into it.
Heat the remaining olive oil in a wok and fry the cubes of ham.
Add the leek and fry briefly. Add the nasi herbs and rice. Fry while stirring.
Beat 3 eggs and make thin omelettes with butter in a frying pan.
Roll them up and cut into strips. Stir them into the nasi. Fry the remaining 4 eggs.
Put the nasi on the plates, together with the chicken in satay sauce and a fried egg and serve with prawn crackers, gherkins, cocktail onions and sambal.

traditional Dutch desserts & pastries

Pancakes with syrup

serves 4

200 g self-raising flour, sieved
pinch of salt
400 ml milk
2 eggs
butter to fry in

Beat the flour, salt, milk and eggs to a smooth batter. Melt a knob of butter in a frying pan and pour in enough batter to cover the base generously. Cook the pancake on a medium heat until the top is almost dry. Turn the pancake and cook this side until golden brown. Drizzle the pancakes with syrup and roll them up.

Mini pancakes with icing sugar

serves 4

250 g self-raising flour, sieved
pinch of salt
350 ml lukewarm milk
1 tsp. sugar
1 egg
melted butter
icing sugar, sieved
knobs of butter

Beat the flour, salt and milk to a smooth batter and add the sugar and the egg while still beating.
Heat a mini pancake tray and grease it with melted butter. Fill the cups for three quarters with batter. Bake the mini pancakes on a medium heat until the top is almost dry and turn the pancakes. Bake this side until golden brown. Put the mini pancakes on a plate, sprinkle generously with icing sugar and put knobs of butter on them.

serves 4

3 egg whites
pinch of salt
125 g sugar
200 ml red currant juice

Haagse bluf

(red currant whip)

Beat the egg whites with the salt until almost stiff. While beating add the sugar gradually until the egg white is completely stiff. Beat the juice into it and continue beating until the mixture is very airy. Divide the mixture between 4 dishes and put a spoon in it. You can also serve it with sponge-fingers or macaroons.

Butter biscuit

makes 1 biscuit

250 g flour, sieved
200 g soft brown sugar
pinch of salt
1 sachet vanilla sugar
225 g cold butter, in cubes
1 egg to glaze

Mix the flour, brown sugar, salt and vanilla sugar and put the cubes of butter on top. Knead quickly to a dough and push the dough into a small greased cake tin.
Smooth the top with a wet spoon.
Glaze the top with the lightly beaten egg and mark out a pattern of squares in the dough.
Bake the butter biscuit in the oven for 15-20 minutes at 220 °C.
Leave to cool in the tin and cut into pieces.

serves 4

2 eggs
150 ml milk
8 slices of (old) white bread
50 g butter
2 tbsp. sugar
2 tsp. cinnamon

Wentelteefjes

(French toast)

Beat the eggs slightly and stir in the milk. Put the slices of bread in the egg mixture and leave to soak briefly.
Melt the butter in a frying pan and fry the bread on both sides until golden brown.
Take the bread out of the pan and keep it warm. Sprinkle the wentelteefjes with sugar and cinnamon. Delicious serving suggestion - bake pieces of apple and place on the wentelteefjes.

Rice pudding

serves 4

1 litre whole milk
150 g pudding rice
pinch of salt
2 sachets of vanilla sugar
1 tsp. cinnamon
1 tsp. nutmeg
1 egg yolk, lightly beaten
1 egg white, stiffly beaten
3 tbsp. dark brown sugar

Bring the milk to the boil in a pan with a thick bottom and stir the rice, salt, vanilla sugar, cinnamon and nutmeg into the milk. Bring to the boil again, put the lid partly back on the pan and simmer for 50-60 minutes to cook the rice. Stir in the egg yolk and the egg white and leave the rice pudding to cool. Sprinkle the brown sugar over the rice pudding.

Also in this series:

Hollands Unlimited!
ISBN 978 90 5964 5981

Japans Unlimited!
ISBN 978 90 5964 4892

Tapas Unlimited!
ISBN 978 90 5964 4854

Wokken Unlimited!
ISBN 978 90 5964 4847

Winterkost Unlimited!
ISBN 978 90 5964 6483

Pasta Unlimited!
ISBN 978 90 5964 4861

Colophon

ISBN 978 90 5964 5202

Text: Francis van Arkel, NutriVisie
Styling: Moniek Visser
Photography: Remco Lassche, Bart Nijs fotografie,
Archive Studio ImageBooks
Lay out: Studio ImageBooks

www.imagebooks.nl